GREG STI

SHARING MY FAITH

REACH OUT

DON'T FREAK OUT

student devotional

Visit our website: simplyyouthministry.com

Credits
Author: Greg Stier
Executive Developer: Nadim Najm
Chief Creative Officer: Joani Schultz
Dare 2 Share Editor: Jane Dratz
Editors: Rob Cunningham and Janis Sampson
Cover Art Director: Jeff A. Storm
Designer: Veronica Lucas
Production Manager: DeAnne Lear

ISBN 978-0-7644-6459-1

10 9 8 7 6 5 4 3 2 1   20 19 18 17 16 15 14 13 12 11

Printed in the United States of America.

DEDICATION

To the thousands of students who've attended Dare 2 Share evangelism training conferences and are sharing their faith and living THE Cause.

CONTENTS

INTRODUCTION

Reaching out to your friends with Jesus' message is something God has called YOU to do! No matter who you are or how scared or unprepared you feel, sharing your faith is central to the purposes God has for you on this earth. Jesus lays it right out there for you in Acts 1:8 when he says, *"And you will be my witnesses, telling people about me everywhere."*

So why not learn how to share your faith with others effectively? After all, sharing Jesus' message is the **most important thing you'll ever do**, both now and for all eternity. Learning how to reach out without freaking out only makes sense.

And that's what this 30-day devo is all about. As you make your way through the following pages of this book, you'll find daily motivation, tips, strategies, and practical exercises that will help you reach your friends.

You'll also discover that you aren't alone on this faith-sharing journey. Jesus goes with you. And thousands of teenagers just like you are walking this road right alongside you. You'll get to "Listen In" on just a few of their true stories in the coming pages. You'll find encouragement and creative ideas in their stories that you can try for yourself as you reach out to your friends.

So face down your fears and step up to this great adventure of sharing your faith with your friends. It will change your life and have impact for all of eternity! Your generation is better connected than any generation in history. You are poised to rock the world for Jesus! But it all starts with learning how to reach out without freaking out.

—Greg Stier

Dare 2 Share

one

CONNECTING

And all of this is a gift from God, who brought us back to himself through Christ. And God has given us this task of reconciling people to him. For God was in Christ, reconciling the world to himself, no longer counting people's sins against them. And he gave us this wonderful message of reconciliation. **(2 Corinthians 5:18-19)**

THE BIG IDEA

Jesus wants your friends to get to know him. Do you want that, too?

LISTEN IN

The pain inside me had been burning my heart into ashes for years. No one knew about this pain. Not my family or friends. I didn't dare let them realize how weak I was. I had many friends, yet every day, I lived a nightmare and I felt so alone. I usually put on a mask—one of great confidence and happiness—and tried to look like I didn't have a care in the world. I succeeded in fooling everyone. No one saw past my mask. That hurt. I used to cry myself to sleep. I felt really pathetic and useless…then I tried to commit suicide… —L

GOING DEEPER

Close your eyes and think about your friends who don't know Jesus. Could one of them have written the words above? Because L is a real person—a young girl who silently struggled to carry on without hope. Like each of the "Listen In" stories that appear in this book, L's story is a true story.

L's account in her own words shows us that we may be surprised by what's actually going on inside our friends who live without the hope Jesus brings. But whether their lives are full of pain or they're happily pursuing stuff that in the end will shrivel up and blow away, the spiritual reality is that they are distant from God. Either way, their lives will be difficult because they will be empty of the great joy that comes from knowing God. And their afterlife will be even more difficult—an eternity spent separated from God in a place the Bible describes as unbearable and unending.

They need to hear about Jesus' offer of salvation and his free gift of a close, personal relationship with God. You hold those words of life. Are you willing to help your friends get connected to God?

DO SOMETHING!

Close your eyes and ask God to bring to mind the name of one friend who needs Jesus. Write that name down in today's journal entry. Then write a note to Jesus about this person and ask him to prepare the way for you to spend some time talking to this friend about Jesus.

Note to Jesus about my friend...

FACING | YOUR FEARS

For God has not given us a spirit of fear and timidity, but of power, love, and self-discipline. So never be ashamed to tell others about our Lord. **(2 Timothy 1:7-8)**

THE BIG IDEA

God has provided truths in his Word that can help you overcome your fears about sharing your faith with your friends.

LISTEN IN

When asked what they fear most about sharing their faith, most teenagers are brutally honest. "My biggest fear is getting rejected by people," one student commented. "That my friends are gonna think I'm weird," another guy chimed in. "That I won't know what to say," volunteered a third, as other heads nodded their agreement. But teenagers seem to agree that their fear of rejection tops the list.

GO DEEPER

Does the idea of bringing God up make you want to throw up? You're not alone. Most Christians seem to wrestle with some fears when it comes to sharing their faith. But God has provided truths in his Word to help you face down your fears!

Here are three of the most common faith-sharing fears:

1. My friends might reject me. Nobody wants to lose friends—yuck! But if you approach your friends with love and concern as you share the gospel, you will reduce your fear of rejection. Still, there's a chance sharing your faith may cause some eye-rolling and strained relationships, because some people find the message of the gospel uncomfortable or even offensive. But take courage because 1 Thessalonians 2:4 tells us: *For we speak as messengers approved by God to be entrusted with the Good News. Our purpose is to please God, not people. He alone examines the motives of our hearts.* When it comes to a choice between pleasing God or pleasing people, which do you think should win out?

2. I'm not a perfect Christian. Do you need to be a "perfect" Christian before you try to talk about Jesus with others? While striving to become more like Jesus is important, 2 Corinthians 4:7 promises that the gospel can shine through us despite our weaknesses and imperfections. It says: *We now have this light shining in our hearts, but we ourselves are like fragile clay jars containing this great treasure. This makes it clear that our great power is from God, not from ourselves.* These words make it clear: it's SOOO not about you—it's about God. It's like someone once said, "Evangelism is just one beggar showing another where to find food." We're far from perfect; we're just trying to help others by introducing them to Jesus.

3. I won't know what to say. Our God is immense. The message of his grace is awesome and mindbending—way beyond our puny brains. It's easy to feel overwhelmed at the prospect of trying to explain God to others. Still, 1 Peter 3:15 challenges you to do just that: *If someone asks about your Christian hope, always be ready to explain it.* So if not knowing what to say has you stressed, no worries—this book is designed to help you learn to share the gospel in a clear and compelling way.

DO SOMETHING!

Think through your own personal fears about sharing your faith. Identify the one that looms largest for you. No matter your fear, God wants to help you face it down. Stand in front of a mirror and read the following passage out loud: *For God has not given us a spirit of fear and timidity, but of power, love, and self-discipline. So never be ashamed to tell others about our Lord (2 Timothy 1:7-8).* Look yourself in the eye and decide whether you believe these verses. Journal today about how you're feeling about facing your fears. Throughout the day, ask God to give you the "power, love, and self-discipline" you need to overcome your fears and share your faith.

How I'm feeling as I face my fears...

PRAYER

the best offense and defense

If the Good News we preach is hidden behind a veil, it is hidden only from people who are perishing. Satan, who is the god of this world, has blinded the minds of those who don't believe. They are unable to see the glorious light of the Good News. They don't understand this message about the glory of Christ, who is the exact likeness of God. **(2 Corinthians 4:3-4)**

THE BIG IDEA

Prayer is mission critical as you share your faith, because you're entering into a spiritual battle for the hearts and souls of your friends.

LISTEN IN

I'm trying to get as many people as possible praying for my close friend who is struggling with the idea of letting Christ into her life. She wants to have a new start, but she is scared. She was in a bad car accident last weekend, and in the back of her head she knows she wouldn't be in heaven right now if she'd died. Please pray that she lets her guard down a bit more and accepts Christ.
—Zeke

GOING DEEPER

When you share the gospel with your friends, you're entering spiritually dangerous territory. To put it bluntly, you're in a battle.

While the God of the universe is extending his offer of grace and salvation to your friends, the forces of darkness seek to keep them bound and blinded from the truth. Jesus defeated Satan by dying on the cross, but Satan and his dark forces haven't surrendered yet. They're still on a rampage to do as much damage as they can before Jesus returns to rule and reign forever.

Your best offensive *and* defensive weapon in this spiritual battle is prayer. Even the Apostle Paul, who you could safely say had his act together when it came to sharing his faith, asked for prayer so he could nail it: *Stay alert and be persistent in your prayers...And pray for me, too. Ask God to give me the right words so I can boldly explain God's mysterious plan (Ephesians 6:18-19).*

This spiritual battle is not won through smooth talk or great debating skills; instead it's won in the heart and soul of each individual. That's why prayer is central.

So plug into the power of the Holy Spirit through prayer, ask God to prepare the hearts of your friends, and then move out into the spiritual battle with courage and conviction. Sharing the gospel is the most eternally impacting thing you'll ever do, so lay the groundwork first and pray, pray, pray!

DO SOMETHING!

Think of that one friend God laid on your heart a couple days ago. Then ask God to expand your vision beyond that one friend—and ask him to call to mind two more friends who don't know Jesus. Write about these three friends in your journal entry today, describing where you think they are spiritually. Then pray specifically for these three friends. Ask God to give you courage and spiritual insight as you seek to reach them with the message of the gospel. Ask God to prepare their hearts for his message. Ask God to protect you from the evil one and guide you as you enter into this bold adventure of sharing your faith.

Three friends who need Jesus...

four⁴

SEIZE | THE MOMENT

I try to find common ground with everyone, doing everything I can to save some **(1 Corinthians 9:22).**

THE BIG IDEA

Look for natural opportunities in the midst of normal conversations to turn the talk toward spiritual things.

LISTEN IN

I shared my faith with a girl in my biology class during a lab. It was so spontaneous, and I almost missed my chance. It all started with a bracelet I was wearing … :) So we talked the entire hour, and yes, we finished the lab. She said she thought doing good deeds would get you to heaven but I explained how it's all about Jesus paying the price for us through his death on the cross. In the end, she smiled and thanked me for the awesome "non-jerk" conversation. She said I was the first Christian she'd had a major conversation with who hadn't tried to shove it down her throat and who listened to her. Today was a great day! —Chris

GO DEEPER

Bringing God up with your friends can be stomach churning. But it can become less nerve racking if you tune in to conversations with an ear toward sharing your faith. Often normal, everyday conversations come with a natural "fork in the road" where someone makes a comment that leaves the door open and gives you an opportunity to move the conversation in a spiritual direction. With prayer and a little focused attention, you can often take the path that opens the way for you to talk about Jesus.

In Chris' conversation, it started with a bracelet comment, but there are many ways to move a conversation toward God. For example, if a friend is talking about feeling hurt, you might say something like "When I'm hurting, one of the things I do is pray." Or if a friend is venting about some relational drama in his or her life right now, you might say something like "Sometimes relationships can be really tough, but the one relationship I can always count on is my relationship with God."

Get your friends talking about their spiritual beliefs. Find common ground when you can, and compliment them on the spiritual beliefs they have right. Ask them if they've ever heard Christianity presented as a relationship instead of a religion. Work to break down the walls that keep people from talking about their spiritual beliefs, and remember that your conversation is never about winning an argument, but a soul.

DO SOMETHING!

Just having your "sharing radar" turned on will tune you in to opportunities to share your faith. In one of your conversations today, look for a way to turn the conversation toward spiritual things. Pray that God will help you be brave, and then seize the moment!

At the end of the day, come back and journal about your efforts. How did it go? What would you do differently? In hindsight, did you miss any opportunities?

How I "seized the moment" today...
or wish I had...

BE RELATIONAL

You're here to be light, bringing out the God-colors in the world. God is not a secret to be kept. We're going public with this, as public as a city on a hill. If I make you light-bearers, you don't think I'm going to hide you under a bucket, do you? I'm putting you on a light stand. Now that I've put you there on a hilltop, on a light stand—shine! Keep open house; be generous with your lives. By opening up to others, you'll prompt people to open up with God, this generous Father in heaven. **(Matthew 5:14-16 The Message)**

THE BIG IDEA

God has placed you in your circle of influence to share his love and gospel message.

LISTEN IN

I posted the following note titled "I'm curious…" and tagged as many friends as possible as a way to kick-start my evangelism:

Umm…OK, this is gonna sound weird but here it goes—

> *All right, I want you all to know I love ya, no matter how you react to the questions I'm about to ask you. And just to get it out of the way, I'm not gonna use this for anything other than the fact that I'm curious. Got it? All right.*

> *I want to know what you all believe. You can answer here or in a private message, it doesn't matter to me. I want to know if you're atheist, agnostic, Muslim, Christian, etc.*

> *If you would like to tell me your basic beliefs as well, that would be awesome :) The message can be as short or as long as you wish, I just want to know. If you don't want*

to talk to me about it beyond your response, you need to let me know 'cause otherwise I will probably at least ask you a few questions. :)

Love you all!

The responses I have been getting blow my mind... —Julie

GO DEEPER

Reread the Bible verses at the beginning of this entry. The Message paraphrase uses some interesting wording that provides a fresh look at these familiar verses about "letting your light shine."

Jesus' way isn't meant to be hidden or secret. He came to earth to proclaim his gift of grace to all humanity, and he left his followers with the responsibility of sharing that message with everyone. When he says, *"Keep open house; be generous with your lives. By opening up to others, you'll prompt people to open up with God...,"* who's he expecting to take the first step here? Are these verses describing you waiting for people to come and ask you about God, or are they describing you taking the initiative and taking his message to others? What better place to start being "generous" and "opening up to others" than in your own circle of friends?

According to the nerd squad, a friend has 100 times more influence on another friend than a stranger does. With prayer and a little preparation, you can do more to impact your friends for Jesus than any stranger ever could. God has planted you in your sphere of influence so you can be a light-bearer and reach into people's lives with his love and his gospel. Whether it's with friends from school, sports, work, or whatever, you are called by Christ to be his light in both word and deed.

DO SOMETHING!

Julie decided to step out into her network of relationships and openly approach the topic of spirituality. Spend a few minutes journaling about your reaction to Julie's approach. Like it? Don't like it? Then step out today and talk about Jesus with at least one friend. Feel free to try Julie's approach, or come up with your own, but either way, do something!

My plan today for talking about spiritual things with my friends...

BE RELENTLESS

Obviously, I'm not trying to win the approval of people, but of God.
If pleasing people were my goal, I would not be Christ's servant.
(Galatians 1:10)

THE BIG IDEA
Sometimes sharing your faith can be uncomfortable, but God calls
us to relationally and relentlessly share his message with others.
And we must seek to please God and not people.

LISTEN IN
We recently decided to have a "do-over" See You at the Pole. Last
fall, there were about five students that came out for the official See
You at the Pole day, and we literally got rocks thrown at us. (Talk
about persecution through stoning!) But we wanted to take another
stand; so this past Wednesday at 7:00 a.m., we gathered again
around the school's flagpole. This time there were 26 students! We
rallied together, prayed, sang worship songs, and even gave devos!
We are responding to God and the call to bring Jesus to our school!
—REASON Youth Church

GO DEEPER
Sometimes sharing your faith can be uncomfortable. It can feel
embarrassing or scary. It can give you palpitations or make you
sweat through your favorite shirt. It can strain your relationships.
It can cost you popularity. Even when you share the gospel in
the most caring way possible, the message of Jesus' free gift of

salvation can bring controversy. In fact, sometimes people who aren't Christians direct their anger or discomfort at the gospel message toward the Christian who is the messenger, even if it is a friend.

But Galatians 1:10 says that as a follower of Jesus, your focus must be on pleasing God and not people. So be relational *and* relentless in your efforts to share your faith. Don't be surprised if you encounter some resistance along the way. But don't give up! Pray for boldness and stay true to the calling that Jesus has given his followers to make disciples.

DO SOMETHING!

Can you remember a time when you sensed God was prompting you to speak up about something but you stayed quiet instead? Ask God to give you the courage and boldness you need to keep that from happening ever again. Determine in your heart and before God to seek to please God and not people in the coming days. Journal about an alternate scenario—how it might unfold differently if you had a do-over. Commit to stepping up and speaking out about the gospel. Then start today by texting or calling one friend to tell them you want to set up a time to talk about God.

If I could do that conversation over,
here's what it'd look like...

seven

BRINGING IT UP

Yet God has made everything beautiful for its own time. He has planted eternity in the human heart, but even so, people cannot see the whole scope of God's work from beginning to end.
(Ecclesiastes 3:11)

THE BIG IDEA

Develop some conversation starters to help you bring God up in conversations with your friends.

LISTEN IN

I texted my friend Jess and asked her where she thought she was going when she died. "I don't know…heaven?" she replied. So I texted back, "Do you want to go to heaven for sure?" "Yeah, but how?" Jess asked. Then I explained the gospel to her and asked her if she would put her trust in Jesus. "I don't know," she texted back. I asked her if she'd sleep on it. She said, "OK." The next morning I texted her again and asked her the same question. She said yes! I just thought, if I can help one of my friends give his or her life to Christ (through texting), just imagine what I can do face-to-face.
—David

GO DEEPER

Sometimes bringing God up in conversation can feel awkward. But don't be intimidated; most teenagers are very open to talking about spiritual things. In fact, a 2010 poll of teenagers ages 13-17 says 71 percent of teenagers pray (barna.org). The fact that teenagers want to connect with God through prayer really shouldn't come as a surprise because Ecclesiastes 3:11 says that God has *"planted eternity in the human heart."* We are all made with a God-shaped hole inside us that only God can fill. By sharing the truth of Jesus' gospel message, you are offering your friends the gift of a relationship with Jesus now and forever.

But how do you actually go about bringing God up? Check out these conversation-starting questions for ideas:

- Do you believe in God?...If there is a God, what do you think he wants from you?...Would it surprise you to learn that God wants a relationship with you?

- I really liked that movie; did you notice all the spiritual themes in it?

- I know you're hurt by what your friend said; do you ever take your hurt feelings to God and ask him how you should respond?

- I'm sorry your Grandma has cancer; does it make you wonder about what it takes to get into heaven when you die?

- That's a sweet song; does that one line ever get you thinking about God when you hear it?

- Did you hear about that terrible accident yesterday? It makes you think about what happens when we die, doesn't it?

- That news story was really disturbing; where do you turn when you're afraid or freaked out?

DO SOMETHING!

Spend some time thinking through some conversation starters you'd be comfortable using. In your journal entry, write down a few you like from the list above, or be creative and come up with your own. Then pick one and post it on your Facebook page today, or use it to initiate a spiritual conversation face to face.

*Spiritual conversation starters
I want to try...*

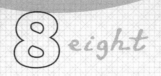

YOU'RE
unique

You made all the delicate, inner parts of my body and knit me together in my mother's womb. Thank you for making me so wonderfully complex! Your workmanship is marvelous—how well I know it. **(Psalm 139:13-14)**

THE BIG IDEA

Understanding that God has uniquely wired you with an individual style of sharing your faith can help you more effectively share the gospel.

LISTEN IN

Zane and I are friends. Both of us are Christians who are committed to sharing our faith with others, but our individual approaches to sharing the gospel are very different. Zane's faith-sharing style centers on building relationships with others and then bringing the gospel up in the context of a safe, trusting relationship. On the other hand, my approach is to talk about spiritual things with others early and often, purposefully engaging them to seriously reflect on their spiritual beliefs and consider the message of the gospel. One approach isn't right and the other wrong, but they are very different.
—Greg

GO DEEPER

Style is a personal thing. If you buy your clothes from Hollister you have one style; if you frequent Hot Topic, you have another. The same is true when it comes to sharing your faith. Your individual faith-sharing "style" is influenced by your God-given personality and your spiritual gifting. When we look at the early church, we can see four faith-sharing styles modeled in the New Testament. I've labeled them like this: talkers, "stalkers," buddies, and brains. In the example above, Zane is a buddy, and I am a talker/"stalker" mix. No one style is better than the others; they are just different approaches. And some people may be a blend of several. In fact, Jesus modeled the ultimate balance of all four styles.

Since understanding how God's wired you with your unique style of sharing can help you be more effective, the next four devos are designed to help you understand each of these four styles. Maybe you'll recognize yourself! Or maybe you're a blend. But regardless of your style, just remember that the most important thing is to lovingly communicate the gospel in the power of the Holy Spirit.

DO SOMETHING!

No matter how God's wired you when it comes to sharing your faith, you can't go wrong doing something nice for a friend and using that act of kindness as a springboard to giving that person the greatest gift of all—a relationship with Jesus. Try it today. Do something generous for a friend, and then talk to that person about how God's been generous with you, and explain Jesus' gift of salvation. Lay some groundwork in your journal entry.

How God's been generous to me...

How I can be generous toward others...

TALKERS | WINSOME AND WORDY

So Paul, standing before the council, addressed them as follows: "Men of Athens, I notice that you are very religious in every way, for as I was walking along I saw your many shrines. And one of your altars had this inscription on it: 'To an Unknown God.' This God, whom you worship without knowing, is the one I'm telling you about. … His purpose was for the nations to seek after God and perhaps feel their way toward him and find him—though he is not far from any one of us. For in him we live and move and exist. As some of your own poets have said, 'We are his offspring.'" **(Acts 17:22-23, 27-28)**

THE BIG IDEA

When it comes to styles of faith-sharing, talkers tend to be winsome and wordy.

LISTEN IN

I set out for school one Monday morning determined to share my faith with at least one person that day. So I'm sitting around talking with friends about college, then it went to family stuff, and then to religion…I knew this was my perfect opportunity (GOD IS AMAZING!), so I said, "Oh, I hate the word RELIGION! I hate it with a passion!" At that point, I was so excited I could barely get the words out, but I explained to my friends that knowing God wasn't about religion. Religion is all about humans trying to earn their way to God. But what God wants is a relationship with us—which is all about what Jesus did. I was so excited that at one point I just blurted out, "Thank you, God!" (My friends got a hoot out of that!)

We ended up having a deep conversation about Jesus, and I even gave away my copy of the book Venti Jesus Please. *(A book that helps nonbelieving teenagers take a closer look at Jesus.)*

I love sharing God with people! It is so awesome! —Allie

GO DEEPER

Talkers tend to be friendly, funny and filled with enthusiasm. They have a contagious excitement for the good news and want the rest of the world to join the party. Allie's excitement in the above recounting practically jumps off the page. Talkers live life in CAPS and exclamation points!!! They are gifted in finding creative and oftentimes funny ways to insert God into their conversations with others, which Allie did in this situation by saying, "Oh, I *hate* the word *religion!*"

In the Bible, the Apostle Paul appears to be a talker. In Acts 17 we find him creating a natural opening and working to connect with his listeners by referring to their gods and their poets. He walks into the opening he's created and quickly moves the conversation toward the message of the gospel.

Talkers like Allie and the Apostle Paul bring their own unique blend of strengths and weaknesses to their faith-sharing efforts. Their strengths include the force of their personality and their natural enthusiasm, both of which help them draw people into spiritual conversations and communicate a persuasive gospel message. One of their weaknesses may be a tendency to talk so much that they don't take time to really listen to others.

DO SOMETHING!

If you're a talker, take some time to journal about how you can maximize your personal strengths and minimize your weaknesses, and then step out and initiate a spiritual conversation with at least one person today. If you aren't a talker, journal about what you can learn from talkers that might help you become more effective as you share your faith, and then try incorporating some of the talker's friendliness and enthusiasm into your efforts today to initiate a spiritual conversation.

Things I can learn from talkers' strengths and weaknesses...

"STALKERS" | BOLD AND DIRECT

That's when Peter stood up and, backed by the other eleven, spoke out with bold urgency: "Fellow Jews, all of you who are visiting Jerusalem, listen carefully and get this story straight...Change your life. Turn to God and be baptized, each of you, in the name of Jesus Christ, so your sins are forgiven. Receive the gift of the Holy Spirit."
(Acts 2:14, 38 The Message)

THE BIG IDEA

A "stalkers" approach to sharing their faith is generally bold, direct, and unflinching.

LISTEN IN

Just a few minutes ago, I started talking to one of my friends. We just wanted something to talk about. And I was like, "Well, do you believe in God?" And we just started talking. We talked about it for about an hour. It was awesome. —Jess

GO DEEPER

"Stalking" in the context of sharing your faith doesn't mean you follow people in the dark of night and badger them incessantly like the paparazzi. This kind of "stalker" refers to individuals who are determined and singular in their goals—focused, bold and unflinching. "Stalkers" are often Type-A personalities who are strong leaders and highly successful in everything from sports to making money.

Like Jess in the above recounting, "stalkers" are assertive and uninhibited, generally willing to jump in with both feet and just bring the subject of God up out of thin air. The Apostle Peter in Acts 2 demonstrates a typical "stalker" sharing style. He boldly and bluntly steps forward with statements like *"Make no mistake about this..."* and *"Change your life. Turn to God."* He unapologetically lays the truth of the gospel out in plain view for all to see.

For "stalkers" like Jess and the Apostle Peter, their strengths include their courage to speak the truth and to be persistent as they share the message of the gospel, urging others to a point of decision about Jesus. One of their weaknesses is their tendency to come on so strong that they sometimes turn people off. Balancing their boldness to proclaim the truth with love and a caring spirit can minimize the turn-off factor.

DO SOMETHING!

If you're a "stalker," journal about how you can maximize your personal strengths and minimize your weaknesses, and then step out and initiate a spiritual conversation with at least one person today. If you aren't a "stalker," journal about what you can learn from "stalkers" about being bolder and more up front when it comes to sharing your faith, and then step out and initiate a spiritual conversation.

Things I can learn from "stalkers'"
strengths and weaknesses...

BUDDIES | FRIENDS FOREVER

Meanwhile, a Jew named Apollos, an eloquent speaker who knew the Scriptures well, had arrived in Ephesus from Alexandria in Egypt. He had been taught the way of the Lord, and he taught others about Jesus with an enthusiastic spirit and with accuracy. However, he knew only about John's baptism. When Priscilla and Aquila heard him preaching boldly in the synagogue, they took him aside and explained the way of God even more accurately. **(Acts 18:24-26)**

THE BIG IDEA

Buddies' natural inclination is to share their faith in the context of a caring relationship.

LISTEN IN

I finally had a conversation about God with my friend where I explained the gospel to her. She said she didn't know if she'd go to heaven if she died and told me that not knowing scared her. So I told her if she believed that Jesus was sent to earth and died on the cross to take away our sins and if she put her trust in him, he would give her everlasting life. After she prayed, she busted out with tears, and she immediately felt relief. She was shocked by the simplicity of it.

Since then her life has changed. Our relationship has gotten stronger now that God is fully part of it. Her attitude has changed, and she is happier all the time. Now she feels that God has a purpose for her. She attends church with me pretty much every Sunday and she loves it! I also gave her a devotional. She loves to learn more about God, and we enjoy learning things together! She is strong in her faith, despite what others think about her choice to become a born-again believer. Words can't describe how far she has come and how strong she is. I am so proud of her, and she is an inspiration to me! —Ashley

GO DEEPER

Buddies like Ashley are relational and caring. They have a huge capacity for loving others and listening. They care deeply when others are hurting or scared and step into that hurt or fear with the message of a loving, merciful, personal God. Buddies sometimes come through the side door rather than the front door when it comes to sharing their faith, letting the conversation unfold as they listen and gently nudge it toward Jesus. In Acts 18, we see Priscilla and Aquila demonstrating buddy behavior through their care and concern for Apollos, taking him aside to explain the gospel of Christ.

Buddies' biggest challenge is their tendency to work so long at building relationships that they chicken out about actually sharing their faith because they're afraid of creating tension in their relationships. Fear of rejection looms particularly large for buddies.

DO SOMETHING!

If you're a buddy, journal today about how you can maximize your personal faith-sharing strengths and minimize your weaknesses. Then step out and initiate a spiritual conversation today. If you aren't a buddy, journal about what you can learn from buddies that might help you become more loving and relational when sharing your faith, and then try incorporating those insights into your efforts to initiate a spiritual conversation today.

Things I can learn from buddies'
strengths and weaknesses...

12 *twelve*

BRAINS | AS A MATTER OF FACT

Having carefully investigated everything from the beginning, I also have decided to write a careful account for you, most honorable Theophilus. **(Luke 1:3)**

THE BIG IDEA

Brains are intellectual and prefer to use a well-reasoned, logical approach in their presentation of the gospel.

LISTEN IN

During silent reading at school, I noticed my friend Chris looked bored with his book, so I told him to read Venti Jesus Please, *which I had in my backpack. (He's not a Christian.) As he read it, he looked like he was actually into it. Usually he looks up and stuff and doesn't really read, but he stayed focused. I think he may be a whole new step closer to God as a result!*

Then, during the next period (which was math), I started having another conversation with two people at my table. One is Muslim and the other atheist. The atheist, Josh, was wondering about the Ten Commandments. Then the Muslim, Ada, started asking me things about Jesus and about why God can't just say, "OK, you can all go to heaven!" so that just like that, our sins would be forgiven. So I explained to her why Jesus had to die on the cross for us. And I was so thankful I had read Venti Jesus Please, *otherwise I don't think I would have been able to answer her. Then my friend Matt, who is a Christian, joined the conversation and to my surprise*

Cameron did, too! I was so excited! I think Cameron might really be interested in Jesus, and I think I got Josh and Ada thinking, too!
—Natalie

GO DEEPER

Brains like Natalie will often nudge their friends to read a book or go to a website that makes a strong case for Christianity, and then follow up by discussing the content with them. Brains like to seek out answers to theological questions in advance so they are prepared for questions that might come their way. And when they don't know the answers, they're generally ready to dig in and do the research.

Jesus' disciple Luke demonstrates the characteristics of a brain. He wrote the book of Luke and the book of Acts, which were personal letters to his friend Theophilus (think Theo, for short). Luke was a real sleuth about investigating his account and got it all down in writing so he could give his friend a logical, well-reasoned description of Jesus' message and ministry.

Brains like Natalie and Luke are strong in intellect and factually convincing. They use logic to explain the claims of Christ and present compelling reasons for belief. Their weaknesses tend to lie in the area of overwhelming people with facts and logic. They can sometimes turn discussions into debates, rather than honest, caring dialogue and may even stretch the truth or make things up so they can "win" the point. Brains can benefit from remembering the old saying, "People don't care how much you know, until they know how much you care."

DO SOMETHING!

If you're a brain, journal about how you can maximize your personal strengths and minimize your weaknesses, and then step out and initiate a spiritual conversation today using your own unique style. If you aren't a brain, journal about what you can learn from brains that might help you become more informed and well-reasoned as you share your faith, and then take the initiative, and bring God up in conversation with at least one person today.

Things I can learn from brains' strengths and weaknesses...

13 *thirteen*

DISCOVERING YOUR STYLE

*But you will receive power when the Holy Spirit comes upon you.
And you will be my witnesses, telling people about me everywhere.*
(Acts 1:8)

THE BIG IDEA
Discover your style of faith-sharing and use it to share the gospel
in the power of the Holy Spirit.

LISTEN IN
*JC excelled at using creative, engaging stories to get people thinking
about God. (A talker?) But sometimes he challenged others' belief
systems boldly, without flinching. (A "stalker"?) Still other times, he
addressed physical or emotional needs before sharing spiritual truth
relationally. (A buddy?) Yet when appropriate, he used logic and
Scripture to make his spiritual point. (A brain?) The perfect balance
of sharing styles—Jesus Christ.*

GO DEEPER
Are you a blend, or do you have one distinct sharing style? You
may already have a strong sense of which style describes you
best, but here's a little nonscientific "test" to help you either
confirm or re-evaluate your initial gut feelings about your unique
faith-sharing style. Circle the answer that applies *most*:

1. Which word describes you best?

> A. Funny
>
> B. Bold
>
> C. Caring
>
> D. Logical

2. "Sometimes I tend to...

> A. joke around too much."
>
> B. hurt feelings with my directness."
>
> C. worry about what others think of me."
>
> D. get frustrated with others who don't get basic logic."

3. Your friends might describe you as...

> A. the life of the party.
>
> B. the leader of the pack.
>
> C. a friend who really listens.
>
> D. the smart kid.

4. "When trying to lead someone to Christ, I would prefer to...

> A. find a creative way (using humor if possible) to bring it up."
>
> B. just bring it up with a direct question."
>
> C. go out for coffee and pray that it naturally comes up in the conversation."
>
> D. share a book or a website that makes a strong, logical case for Christianity, and then talk about it."

5. "I tend to get in trouble for...

      A. too much joking."

      B. being too blunt."

      C. not much."

      D. arguing."

6. Which phrase best describes your sharing style?

      A. Hey, bro! Listen to this!

      B. Are you talking to me? Good, 'cause I wanna talk to you!

      C. God gave us two ears and one mouth for a reason...to listen first!

      D. Resistance to my logic is futile!

Add up your score: Number of As ___, Bs ___, Cs ___, Ds ___.

Mostly As? Talkers are funny, creative, and "the life of the party" when it comes to sharing Jesus.

Mostly Bs? "Stalkers" are direct, bold, and "the leader of the pack" in their faith-sharing.

Mostly Cs? Buddies are relational and kind when it comes to telling others about Jesus.

Mostly Ds? Brains are smart and logical, making a strong case for Christianity.

DO SOMETHING!

Using your own unique style, and in the power of the Holy Spirit, share your faith with a friend today. If you're a talker, look for a funny, creative way to turn the conversation toward God—online or in real life. If you're a "stalker," use your boldness to just jump in and bring God up. If you're a buddy, try buying a friend a beverage and then turn the conversation toward Jesus—the ultimate Thirst Quencher. If you're a brain, ask a friend some spiritually probing questions and then dialogue about God, all the while standing ready to share a book or website that may help point him or her toward Jesus. And remember, you can always draw from other styles for fresh ideas and approaches.

YOUR STORY

The woman left her water jar beside the well and ran back to the village, telling everyone, "Come and see a man who told me everything I ever did! Could he possibly be the Messiah?" So the people came streaming from the village to see him. **(John 4:28-30)**

THE BIG IDEA

No matter your own unique style of sharing as you engage in spiritual conversations, be prepared to tell your own personal faith story describing how you came to faith in Jesus.

LISTEN IN

She was a loser by most people's standards—five past marriages and one current immoral relationship. Clearly she was trying to fill the God-shaped hole inside her with one failed relationship after another. Yet her powerful inner thirst for something more was unquenched. So when Jesus entered her world, offering her the Living Water of a restored relationship with God and eternal life, she was ready to listen. We know her today as the Samaritan woman or the woman at the well—someone thirsty for more.

GO DEEPER

The woman at the well did more than seek to satisfy her own spiritual thirst. Once she encountered Jesus, she ran back to her village to tell everyone about him, even though she was definitely not part of the in-crowd. John 4:39 tells us that many others believed because of her testimony. And just as she shared with others her experience of Jesus, you, too, should be ready to talk about your own faith story. Even if your friends are skeptical about the message of the gospel, it's hard for them to argue about your own experience when it comes to your personal relationship with Jesus. So while they may think you're a wingnut, they can't very well say, "No way you think/feel/experience/believe that."

DO SOMETHING!

Sharing your faith story effectively involves some preparation. Use the following "Before-and-After Factor" graph as a guide and prepare a concise account of your personal journey to Jesus.

Before Describe how your life was before you met Jesus. What did you struggle with? What were you looking for?	**After** Describe how your life's been since you trusted Jesus. What have you left behind? How do you feel? What have you gained? Be authentic!	**Factor** What were the faith factors in your trusting Jesus? What individuals, feelings or circumstances triggered faith in your heart?

Once you've mapped out your own personal "Before-and-After Factor" (p. 44) tell your own faith story to a friend who needs to hear about Jesus. You can even tell them you have an assignment of "practicing" telling your story and ask them if they'll help you out by listening. Your goal is to keep it brief, but impacting. Ask for honest feedback on how your story impacted your friend, and invite constructive criticism. Pray for your "practice" to yield some significant spiritual conversation about Jesus.

My Before-and-After Factor

Before

After

Factor

GOD CREATED US

to be with him

In the beginning God created the heavens and the earth...The Lord God placed the man in the Garden of Eden to tend and watch over it. **(Genesis 1:1; 2:15)**

THE BIG IDEA

Sharing the gospel with someone is like taking that person on a journey through the story of the Bible. To help you remember the key stops along the way, this journey can be explained in a six-letter acrostic that spells out the word *GOSPEL*. The first stop on the GOSPEL Journey explains that God wants us to be in relationship with him.

LISTEN IN

Wide-eyed and awestruck, Adam and Eve gazed at their beautiful surroundings. The dew-kissed flowers, the songbirds, the splendor of the buck and doe grazing in the meadow all reflected their Creator's deep love for them. Their Maker gave them the purpose and privilege of enjoying and caring for the garden. And in the cool of the evening their Creator walked in the garden with them, eager to share from his heart his great hopes and dreams for them.

GOING DEEPER

God created the universe and everything in it, including the first man and woman, Adam and Eve. God created them to be in perfect relationship with him, with each other, and with creation.

They had no sin, no shame, and nothing to hide before God or each other. The only command God gave to them was not to eat from the fruit of the tree of the knowledge of good and evil.

In the same way, God created each of us to be in absolute and perfect relationship with him and with each other. But that plan was disrupted. To be continued...

DO SOMETHING!

Write the letters G-O-S-P-E-L vertically down the left side of a small card. Next to G write:

> **G**od created us to be with him. (Genesis 1–2)

Put the card somewhere you will see it throughout the day and memorize the **G**.

As you learn each of the six key points of the GOSPEL Journey message in coming days, keep in mind that the GOSPEL Journey acrostic is not designed to be a script you regurgitate to your friends. Instead, think of it as a guide to help you cover the basics of the gospel message in your spiritual conversations.

Talk to one friend today about the amazing truth that the God of the universe wants to be in relationship with each of us.

Knowing that God created me to be
with him makes me feel...

OUR SINS | SEPARATE US FROM GOD

*When Adam sinned, sin entered the world. Adam's sin brought
death, so death spread to everyone, for everyone sinned.*
(Romans 5:12)

THE BIG IDEA

Bad things happen because something went wrong with the world
and with people—that something is called sin, and it separates us
from God.

LISTEN IN

*Stephén was a wild, proud, loud, Wiccan. When asked to think of
one thing he had done in the last 12 months that he was ashamed
of, he was completely honest and vulnerable. Surprisingly, he shared
how guilty he felt, how much he sensed that he was a sinner. This
was significant—because a typical Wiccan doesn't believe in sin.
But in that moment Stephén realized he was guilty and, for the first
time, began to realize that he needed forgiveness from God.*

GO DEEPER

The word *sin* means "to miss the mark." Everyone who's ever
lived (except Jesus) has missed the mark and done things they
feel guilty about. Why is that? The Bible tells us it is because we
live in a fallen world where humans have the free will to choose
to turn toward God or away from him. Sometimes it's difficult to
understand why God has given us this ability to choose between
right and wrong. It's an incredible yet terrifying gift. Adam and

Eve were the first people to abuse the gift. And ever since then, people have been choosing evil and hurting others in small and big ways—from broken promises to mass murder.

Maybe you've wondered why God gave us this ability to sin against him and each other. God gave us this freedom because he created us to be in a relationship with him, and a loving relationship only comes from sincere, freely made choices. But each of us has to make a choice—whether to seek a restored relationship with God or turn our back on him. To be continued...

DO SOMETHING!

Yesterday you wrote out the letters G-O-S-P-E-L on a card. Today, next to O write:

>**O**ur sins separate us from God. (Genesis 3)

Review the **G** part of the GOSPEL Journey from yesterday, and then memorize the **O**. Put the card somewhere you will see it throughout the day. Then initiate a spiritual conversation today with one friend by asking: "What do you do when you feel guilty about something?" Listen, and then explain the forgiveness you've found in Jesus.

Knowing our sins separate us from God makes me feel...

17 *seventeen*

SINS CANNOT BE
removed by good deeds

We are all infected and impure with sin. When we display our righteous deeds, they are nothing but filthy rags. Like autumn leaves, we wither and fall, and our sins sweep us away like the wind. **(Isaiah 64:6)**

THE BIG IDEA
The good things we do can't cover up the fact that we all miss the mark and fall short of God's perfect standard.

LISTEN IN
Imagine you're hosting a birthday party for your friend and you're determined to bake the cake for the party yourself. Things are crazy the afternoon of the party and you get distracted and burn the cake—badly. There's no time to bake another cake, so you decide to cover up the fact that it is burnt by covering it up with frosting. You even write "Happy Birthday" across the top in big, bold letters. At the party, your friend takes one bite, gags, and spits it out. Clearly, the fancy frosting didn't change the awful reality that down underneath, the cake is ruined.

GO DEEPER
Many people think they can earn their way into heaven by "being good." They believe they can cover up their bad deeds with a "frosting" of good deeds. But covering our sinful lives with good deeds doesn't change the fact that we have sinned any more than

frosting can change the reality of a burnt cake. God sees right through the "frosting" straight to our sin.

The Bible tells us that through our own efforts, we can never be good enough to make it into a perfect heaven. James 2:10 says: *For the person who keeps all of the laws except one is as guilty as a person who has broken all of God's laws.* Our holy and perfect God doesn't weigh our good deeds and bad deeds on a scale to see if we can muster up a 51 percent score. God doesn't even grade on the curve! Perfection is God's standard. Sound discouraging? Wait, there's more! To be continued...

DO SOMETHING!

Grab your GOSPEL Journey message card. Next to the S write:

> **S**ins cannot be removed by good deeds. (Genesis 4–
> Malachi 4)

Review the **G** and **O** parts of the GOSPEL Journey, and then memorize the **S** line. Put the card somewhere you will see it throughout the day. Then initiate a spiritual conversation today with one friend by asking: "Do you think it's possible to earn your way into heaven?" Listen, and then explain what the Bible has to say about God's perfect standard.

Knowing sins cannot be removed by good deeds makes me feel...

PAYING THE PRICE FOR SIN

JESUS DIED AND ROSE AGAIN

For God presented Jesus as the sacrifice for sin. People are made right with God when they believe that Jesus sacrificed his life, shedding his blood. **(Romans 3:25)**

THE BIG IDEA

Out of God's great love and justice, Jesus took the penalty of our sin upon himself by dying on the cross.

LISTEN IN

Ben and his mom were shopping at the mall. One minute they were casually looking through a couple racks of guys' shirts, and the next minute the world came crashing down. Out of nowhere, a pickup truck came barreling through the store's window at full speed. In the split second between recognition and impact, Ben's mom leapt toward Ben to push him out of the way. In doing so she placed herself in the path of the oncoming truck. Ben was pushed aside, out of the path of the truck's deadly destruction. His mom, however, was killed instantly. She had sacrificed her life for her son's.

GO DEEPER

The Bible says that God's anger over sin was headed full speed at you. But out of his great love for you, Christ pushed you out of the way, sacrificing his life so you could have a restored relationship with God now and live forever with him in heaven. Jesus died in your place!

Why did blood have to be shed to make us right with God? Because God's holiness and justice demand that a penalty be paid for sin. Hebrews 9:22 says this: *Without the shedding of blood, there is no forgiveness.* In Old Testament times, an innocent lamb was slaughtered for the forgiveness of sins. But then the long-awaited Messiah, Jesus Christ, the Lamb of God, came to earth to be sacrificed on the cross and pay the penalty for our sins. Through Jesus' death and resurrection, the path was opened for our sin to be obliterated. To be continued...

DO SOMETHING!

Grab your GOSPEL Journey message card. Next to the P write:

> **P**aying the price for sin, Jesus died and rose again. (Matthew–Luke)

Review the **G**, **O**, and **S** parts of the GOSPEL Journey, and then memorize the **P**. Then initiate a spiritual conversation today with one friend by asking: "Who do you think Jesus was, and why did he die on the cross?" Listen, and then explain what the Bible has to say about Jesus' great love for us and his willingness to sacrifice his life and pay our penalty.

Knowing that paying the price for sin Jesus died and rose again makes me feel...

19 *nineteen*

EVERYONE WHO TRUSTS IN HIM ALONE HAS ETERNAL LIFE

We are made right with God by placing our faith in Jesus Christ. And this is true for everyone who believes, no matter who we are. For everyone has sinned; we all fall short of God's glorious standard. Yet God, with undeserved kindness, declares that we are righteous. He did this through Christ Jesus when he freed us from the penalty for our sins. **(Romans 3:22-24)**

THE BIG IDEA
Believing in Jesus means you are fully relying on him alone to forgive you for all your sins and give you eternal life.

LISTEN IN
Bryan loved rappelling. The higher the rock face he descended, the bigger the thrill. To go over the edge of a cliff hundreds of feet in the air, dangling by a single rope, required total faith in his equipment. In the end, it all came down to trusting the anchor point and his rope. After all, his very life depended on it.

GO DEEPER
What's the anchor point in your life? What are you trusting in to give you eternal life in the forever after, as well as purpose and meaning in the here and now? The Bible tells us that the anchor point of our life must be Jesus. We must believe in him and trust in him. In fact, the book of John uses the word "believe" 98 times, mostly to describe the way to heaven. The way the Bible uses the

word *believe*, it doesn't simply mean an intellectual understanding and agreement; it actually means "to trust in, to rely upon completely." Believing in Jesus takes more than knowing in your head that Jesus is God, for even Satan knows this truth. Believing in Jesus means you are fully relying on him alone to forgive you for all your sins. It means you are willing to trust him to rescue you completely from sin and its devasting consequences.

DO SOMETHING!

Grab your GOSPEL Journey message card. Next to the E write:

> **E**veryone who trust in him alone has eternal life. (John)

Review the lines of the GOSPEL Journey you've already learned and memorize the **E** part. Then initiate a spiritual conversation today with one friend by asking: "If you died today, do you know for sure that you would go to heaven? Would you like to know what the Bible says about this?" Listen, and then explain what the Bible has to say about trusting in Jesus.

Knowing that everyone who trusts in Jesus alone has eternal life makes me feel...

20 *twenty*

LIFE WITH JESUS
starts now and lasts forever

And this is the way to have eternal life—to know you, the only true God, and Jesus Christ, the one you sent to earth. **(John 17:3).**

The thief's purpose is to steal and kill and destroy. My purpose is to give them a rich and satisfying life...I give them eternal life, and they will never perish. No one can snatch them away from me. **(John 10:10, 28)**

THE BIG IDEA
Eternal life begins the moment you believe and is a personal and permanent relationship with God.

LISTEN IN
You saved my life by sharing the message of the gospel with me. I don't have much, but now I have everything that matters—eternal life. You saved my life by helping me find Jesus' forgiveness for all the horrendous things I've done—my abortion, the drugs, and lots more. And his forgiveness allows me to forgive myself...Thank you. —S

GO DEEPER
S trusted in Jesus and received the free gift of eternal life because someone bothered to share the message of the gospel with her in a way she could understand. The impact on her life was both immediate and eternal. Both her quality and quantity of life were changed through her new faith in Jesus.

S was not just saved from hell (which is good thing and a very big deal); she also entered into a beautiful relationship with a brand-new spiritual Daddy. Through Jesus, she now has free access to the very throne room of the God of the universe. She can talk to him anytime of the day or night, no matter how far she has fallen, no matter where she is or who she is with. And God talks to her as well, through the love letter of his Bible, helping her discover how to please him and how to serve him in the midst of this new, exciting relationship.

DO SOMETHING!

Grab your GOSPEL Journey message card. Next to the L write:

> **L**ife with Jesus starts now and lasts forever. (Acts– Revelation)

Review the lines of the GOSPEL Journey you've already learned and memorize the **L** part. Then initiate a spiritual conversation today with one friend by asking: "What do you think God wants from you? Would it surprise you to learn that God wants a relationship with you that starts now and lasts forever?" Listen, and then share the gospel.

GOSPEL Journey

God created us to be with him.

Our sins separate us from God.

Sins cannot be removed by good deeds.

Paying the price for sin, Jesus died and rose again.

Everyone who trusts in him alone has eternal life.

Life with Jesus starts now and lasts forever.

Knowing life with Jesus starts now and lasts forever makes me feel...

MAKE | THE SONG YOUR OWN

Instead, you must worship Christ as Lord of your life. And if someone asks about your Christian hope, always be ready to explain it. But do this in a gentle and respectful way. **(1 Peter 3:15-16)**

THE BIG IDEA

Use the six GOSPEL Journey stops as a guide and not a script to explain the gospel as you engage in spiritual conversations.

LISTEN IN

Katelin was online when the opportunity to share the gospel dropped into her lap, so she took it. The Facebook conversation was about Jesus. Katelin stepped up and shared the core essentials of the GOSPEL Journey message, using her own words. Here's what she posted:

> *Jesus is fully God because he created the entire world and everyone in it. He loves you and is ALWAYS with you; even if you do something that you think is too bad to be forgiven, he will forgive you. He's fully man because he came to earth and lived a life without ever doing ANYTHING wrong. Then, he died the worst possible death on the cross to take the blame for all the things that we do wrong, since it's impossible for us to live a sinless life. He died a death that he didn't deserve as a payment for everything we've ever done wrong. Then he came BACK to life three days later and ascended into heaven. But he really wants to have a personal relationship with you…if you believe this…pray and tell him that you do so you can spend eternity with him in heaven.*

GO DEEPER

Did you recognize the GOSPEL Journey message behind Katelin's words? It's there, if you look for it.

Learning the GOSPEL Journey is much like putting in the prep work needed to play a guitar. First you learn the chords. Chords give you the basics you need to be creative and play your own personal, powerful music. Similarly, the GOSPEL provides you the basics you need to share the gospel personally and powerfully. Let the Holy Spirit inspire you as you tell people about the gospel in the midst of genuine, relational, give-and-take conversation.

DO SOMETHING!

You've memorized the key points of the GOSPEL Journey message. Now it's time to take these basic "chords" and make them your own as you explain the whole message of the gospel. Remember, it's not a script. In your journal entry, write the GOSPEL Journey message out in your own words, telling the story your way, but covering the six key stops along the way. Then talk with a friend today who doesn't know Jesus, and try incorporating the entire content of the GOSPEL Journey as a guide for your conversation. But don't sweat it; if you have a brain freeze and forget everything else, just remember the cross of Christ and your own story about *your* spiritual journey!

Here's how I'd tell a friend about the GOSPEL Journey message in my own words...

22 *twenty-two*

THE | CAUSE OF CHRIST

For the Son of Man came to seek and save those who are lost.
(Luke 19:10)

THE BIG IDEA

In a world filled with many good and worthy causes, there's one cause that should rise to the top. It's the cause of causes: THE Cause of Christ—making disciples who make disciples.

LISTEN IN

I believe that living out THE Cause at school is important because Jesus told us that we should be making disciples who make disciples. In Ephesians 5 it says that we should be imitators of God and that we should live a life of love, just as Jesus loved us. Last school year I made a commitment to love everyone just as Jesus loved us. I'm glad I made it, and I try my hardest to stay true to it. THE Cause of making disciples who make disciples has become a huge part of my life. Living it out and sharing it with others is an amazing opportunity that I enjoy taking. Just being a Christian who isn't ashamed of the gospel is a battle sometimes...but I'm willing to go where I'm sent. —Katelyn

GO DEEPER

Go Green! No More Bullies! Stop Human Trafficking! You live in a cause-centric world. Many of the causes bombarding you are good and worthy causes. But there's one cause that should rise to the top, demanding your attention, passion, and action. What is this one overarching cause? It's the cause of causes: THE Cause of Christ—making disciples who make disciples.

Committing to THE Cause and sharing Christ with your friends takes hardcore determination. But answering Jesus' clear call to *"make disciples"* is the most important and world-impacting thing you will ever do. If you want to make a difference that starts now and lasts for all eternity, then it's time to make THE Cause of Christ your cause! It is the one overarching cause that can do the most to bring God's grace, truth, and justice to a broken and hurting world.

Just imagine how the world would be different if we all lived by Jesus' twin commands to love God and love others. The evils of this world—like selfishness, greed, broken relationships, hunger, disease, and injustice—could be pushed back if Jesus' followers got serious about sharing him and serving him. The ultimate demonstration of your love for others happens when you do all you can to rescue them from spiritual darkness.

By God's grace and through the power of his Holy Spirit, you can push back the pain of a broken world and the consequences of an eternity separated from God, one life at a time, by introducing others to Jesus!

DO SOMETHING!

Do you want to be like Jesus? Do you *really* want to be like Jesus? If you do, then your heart should burn for the things he was passionate about. Reread the Bible verse that appears at the beginning of this entry. What was Jesus passionate about?

Spend some time right now talking to Jesus about your level of commitment to his cause—THE Cause. Then, if you're ready to commit, sign on the line on page 68 as a promise to God.

Dear God, I believe you've called your followers to THE Cause of making disciples who make disciples. Right now, I commit to living out THE Cause in my life. I will seek to use the unique gifts and personality you have given me to share the gospel with others.

Signed: _____

Date: _____

For specific ideas and encouragement on how to live THE Cause at your school, go to dare2share.org/thecause or facebook.com/livethecause.

THE CAUSE CIRCLE

The Holy Spirit said to Philip, "Go over and walk along beside the carriage." Philip ran over and heard the man reading from the prophet Isaiah. Philip asked, "Do you understand what you are reading?" The man replied, "How can I, unless someone instructs me?" And he urged Philip to come up into the carriage and sit with him..."Tell me, was the prophet talking about himself or someone else?" So beginning with this same Scripture, Philip told him the Good News about Jesus. **(Acts 8:29-31, 34-35)**

THE BIG IDEA

THE Cause Circle is a simple tool designed to help you identify your friends who need Jesus, and to remind you to pray, to pursue spiritual conversations, and to persuade them to consider Jesus' message.

LISTEN IN

Guess what? Today, during a lunch table conversation with my group of friends the topic of Jesus and Christianity came up, just like that! I did my best to seize the opportunity and talk about the GOSPEL Journey message, and I think it went pretty well. One of my friends in particular (the one friend from my Cause Circle I had decided to focus first on reaching), had a lot of incorrect ideas about Christianity and I was able to clear some things up for her. And none of my friends even tried to change the subject! —Lauren

GO DEEPER

In Acts 8, we see Philip explaining the gospel to someone God prompted him to talk to. Similarly, Lauren's story shows her focusing in on reaching her friend and explaining the gospel.

Maybe you're a self-starter who doesn't need help keeping your focus, but if you're like most teenagers with a crazy, busy life, adding a little structure to your faith-sharing efforts may help amp up your impact. Below you'll find THE Cause Circle Lauren mentioned in her story. It's a quick and easy tool designed to help you identify your friends who need Jesus and then stay focused as you pray, pursue spiritual conversations, and persuade them to consider Jesus' message.

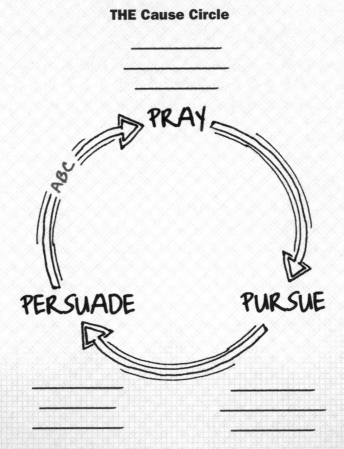

THE Cause Circle

PRAY

PURSUE

PERSUADE

ABC

Here's how it works. Write the names of your friends who need Jesus in the center of the circle. Then place the names of the three friends God has laid on your heart in the "pray" section of the circle. As you have opportunities to pursue spiritual conversations with these friends, advance each name on to the "pursue" area of the circle. Then go back and replace each name in the "pray" section with another friend's name. When you have opportunities to go deeper in your spiritual conversations with your friends, move them forward along the circle to the "persuade" section. What are the ABCs you're working to persuade them of?

- **A**ccept Christ
- **B**elong to a Church
- **C**ommit to THE Cause

In the next three devos, we'll be taking a closer look at each of the three key elements of THE Cause Circle—pray, pursue, persuade—so stay tuned!

DO SOMETHING!

Remember, a nerd squad of researchers recently found that you have 100 times more influence on your friends than a stranger does! God has put you in your friends' lives for a reason!

Pray. Then write the names of your friends who need Jesus in the middle of your Cause Circle. Place the names of those you've been focusing on first in the pray, pursue, and persuade sections, depending on where you are with them. Talk to God about how your efforts to share your faith have been going so far, and ask for courage and insight on where to go from here. Then talk to one of the friends in your circle about Jesus today.

PRAY

Devote yourselves to prayer with an alert mind and a thankful heart. Pray for us, too, that God will give us many opportunities to speak about his mysterious plan concerning Christ. **(Colossians 4:2-3)**

THE BIG IDEA

Prayer is the essential starting point in your efforts to reach your friends because you are engaging in a spiritual battle for their souls.

LISTEN IN

Along with seven of her friends, Tori launched a group that gathers weekly to pray for their school. Together the group has worked hard to get the word out, using word of mouth and youth group announcements to recruit more students. Attendance varies, but at their peak, 50 people showed up to pray!

Still it hasn't all been easy. One week a student who referred to himself as Lucifer disrupted their gathering by cursing and yelling and mocking them. Tori and two of her friends approached the student and responded with kindness, explaining that they just wanted to tell him that Jesus loved him. The angry student continued his string of expletives, but unknowingly threw in a hidden compliment when he complained, "You &$!#% Christians and your niceness—why can't you ever just be jerks back to me?" Tori's response? "Jesus wouldn't treat you that way, so why would I?"

GO DEEPER

Something mysterious happens in the spiritual realm when you pray. While no one can map prayer out like an "if/then" formula or explain it with human logic, Jesus tells his followers to pray and to pray specifically for God's kingdom to come. If you want to see God's kingdom come in the hearts of your friends who need Jesus, prayer is the starting point.

The Bible makes it clear that pulling your friends *out of the darkness into his wonderful light* (1 Peter 2:9) is a spiritual battle that goes far beyond any polished words you might say or logical arguments you might pull out. It is the Spirit of God who convicts your friends of their need for a Savior and convinces them that Jesus is who he claimed to be. Make no mistake. You are engaged in a spiritual battle. A famous old Christian dude named Samuel Chadwick put it this way: "He [Satan] laughs at our toil, mocks at our wisdom, but trembles when we pray."

In Colossians 4:2-3, Paul says that prayer opens doors. Are you willing to put in the hard work of going before God on behalf of your friends' souls? Are you willing to pray for your school like Tori and her friends? Are you ready to armor yourself up through prayer so that you're prepared for the challenges and obstacles the evil one will hurl your way as you enter the spiritual battle for the souls of your friends?

DO SOMETHING!

Write out a prayer to God about your friends who don't know Jesus. Ask God to give you a heart that breaks for them. Ask God for courage, wisdom, and spiritual protection as you pursue spiritual conversations with them. Ask God to open a door for his message in their hearts and minds. Ask God to teach you how to be relational *and* relentless as you share Jesus' message with love and compassion.

Dear God...

25 twenty-five

PURSUE

And he gave us this wonderful message of reconciliation. So we are Christ's ambassadors; God is making his appeal through us. We speak for Christ when we plead, "Come back to God!"
(2 Corinthians 5:19-20)

THE BIG IDEA
Pursuing your friends spiritually means taking the path that moves conversations toward spiritual things.

LISTEN IN
Last weekend I was challenged to share the GOSPEL message with my friends. So I talked to a very good friend of mine via text, and though we haven't finished our conversation and he hasn't come to Christ yet, I was able to share the story of Jesus and his death and what that meant for us. This was something he had never heard before. Now that I know how to explain the GOSPEL, I have more courage to do it, and I will continue to live for THE Cause. —Brianna

GO DEEPER
Reread the verses at the top of this entry. What do you think? Are you supposed to be active or passive in your role of reconciling people to God? The Apostle Paul's words—*We speak for Christ when we plead, "Come back to God!"*—practically shout the need to get out there and pursue friends who need Jesus. Brianna's story of texting her friend shows one way to pursue a friend and get the conversation started.

It's up to you to pick your own approach for actively and urgently pursuing your friends spiritually. But whatever your style, keep your evangelism radar turned on and take the path that moves conversations toward spiritual things. Here are a few examples of what this might look like:

Everyday Situations

- You seem like you're really worried about_____. Are you?...When I'm feeling stressed, I don't know what I'd do if I didn't have my faith in Jesus. He's promised to always be there and walk beside me through the tough stuff. And he promises that for you too if...

- How are you going to decide about_____?...When I have a big decision ahead, it really helps me if I pray about it...Would it be OK with you if I prayed for you about this?

Trends in the Culture

- That was an interesting movie. Do you think there's any truth in how it depicted the supernatural stuff?

- I like that song. It touches something inside me. Sorta like how I feel when I see a beautiful sunset. It makes me think about God and how much he loves us...

- It seems like there's so much bad news in the world—earthquakes, terrorists, and environmental and economic troubles. Does it ever make you wonder if someday everything's just going to implode and Jesus will come back?

Direct Questions

- Do you think there's a spiritual dimension to life?

- I'm curious; can you tell me about your view of God?

- Do you believe in God?...If there is a God, what do you think he wants from you?...Would it surprise you to learn that God wants a relationship with you?

DO SOMETHING!

Take the path toward more spiritual conversations today! In your journal entry, write down a couple questions you plan to use to pursue your friends and bring God up. Use some of the examples above or create your own. Then step out today and launch into one spiritual conversation with a friend.

Questions to use...

PERSUADE

Agrippa interrupted him. "Do you think you can persuade me to become a Christian so quickly?" Paul replied, "Whether quickly or not, I pray to God that both you and everyone here in this audience might become the same as I am, except for these chains."
(Acts 26:28-29)

THE BIG IDEA
Be relational and relentless as you work to persuade your friends to **A**ccept Christ, **B**elong to a Church, and **C**ommit to THE Cause.

LISTEN IN
I shared the gospel with my friend Aaron today. It was perfect timing and everything. It was just us, and I just said out of the blue, "If you were to die today…would you know…for sure…if you would go to heaven?" I was stuttering and sweating but something inside of me made me say it…the Holy Spirit. Anyway, we started talking about it, and he said that no, he didn't think he was going to heaven, but he seemed open, so I prayed that God would help and give me courage as I explained the gospel.

We kept talking for a good 30 minutes. It was awesome, amazing. I realized that people really do want to talk about spiritual things; people really do want to know what goes on after life on this earth. I'm a talker, so it was definitely a challenge to sit and listen to Aaron. But I did, and then I shared the GOSPEL message with him. Then later that day he sent me a text saying, "I just wanted to tell you that it was good talking with you. I don't really have anyone to talk to about that stuff." I have first period with him tomorrow, and I have a feeling it's going to come up again. —Luke

GO DEEPER

The "persuade" part of THE Cause Circle involves clearly presenting the gospel and asking your friends to make a decision about Jesus. Don't be afraid to persuade! The Greek word *peitho* means to "make friends of, to win one's favor, gain one's good will, or to seek to win one." It is used eight times in the New Testament in connection with evangelism.

But what exactly are you trying to relationally and relentlessly persuade others to consider? The ABCs referred to in THE Cause Circle diagram stand for persuading others to:

- **A**ccept Christ
- **B**elong to a Church
- **C**ommit to THE Cause

Obviously making disciples starts with the "A" of accepting Christ. After you share the message of the gospel, try asking your friends two simple questions:

- Does that make sense? (If not, explain it again.)
- Is there anything holding you back from putting your faith in Jesus right now?

The moment your friends trust in Jesus, they enter into an unbreakable relationship with God. Their lives will never be the same! But your job doesn't stop there. After they trust Christ, they need help growing in their new relationship with God—that's why the "B" of belonging to a church is important. In the midst of other Christians, they will learn about God's Word and how to walk closely with Jesus.

And finally the "C" of committing to THE Cause will launch newbies into the great adventure of, in turn, sharing their faith with *their* friends. Moving your friends through these ABCs will carry the gospel on and on as it is multiplied out in life after life across school campuses and networks of friends until it rocks the world!

DO SOMETHING!

You've been praying for your friends, you've been initiating spiritual conversations, and you've learned how to tell your story and how to tell God's story using the GOSPEL Journey message. Step out today and unleash your powers of persuasion on one of your friends by encouraging that friend to consider Christ.

27 *twenty-seven*

IMPACT^{100}

Therefore, go and make disciples of all the nations, baptizing them in the name of the Father and the Son and the Holy Spirit. Teach these new disciples to obey all the commands I have given you. And be sure of this: I am with you always, even to the end of the age. **(Matthew 28:19-20)**

THE BIG IDEA

Making disciples who make disciples results in an exponential impact for God's kingdom.

LISTEN IN

I called my friend Brittany to talk about God. She knew about God, but she didn't know God as a friend and Savior, so I told her about him a little, but then she had to go. About 15 minutes later she called me back and said she wanted to learn more! I was sooooo happy! So we got to talking, and she accepted Jesus on the phone that night! I was soooo excited, because she's my best friend! But that was just the beginning. After that, Brit led her mom and dad and two sisters to Christ...she told me that I planted the seed that grew and grew and grew. —Erin

GO DEEPER

If someone offered you a cool million dollars flat out, would you jump at it? Duh! But say they also gave you the option of doubling your money for 30 days, starting with one cent on day one, then two cents on day two, four cents on day three, and so on out to day 30. Which would you choose—the cool million or the modest little doubling penny?

If you chose the million, you'd have chosen poorly! Because the exponential impact of a single penny doubled every day for 30 days yields $5,368,709.12!

Now picture that principle in the spiritual realm. If you led someone to Christ on day one, and then the two of you each led someone to Christ on day two, that would be four followers of Christ. On day three, if each of you reached one other person, that would be eight. After just 30 days of multiplying, there would be 5,368,709 new Christians who would be living in light of the hope of heaven! The exponential impact of multiplying disciples who make disciples is mind boggling!

The book of Acts gives us a glimpse of this same exponential impact. The message of salvation was unleashed by Jesus' command to go and make disciples. His band of followers carried his message far and wide, and it multiplied out across cities and countries until a whole region of the world was turned upside down—and it changed the course of history.

You also get a glimpse of the exponential impact of the gospel being played out in Erin's story above. She led Brittany to Christ, who in turn, led four of her family to Christ. If each of them introduced someone else to Jesus, that would make eight, and on and on. But it all started with Erin's first step of sharing her faith with her best friend.

DO SOMETHING!

You, too, can have exponential impact on your world by helping those you lead to Jesus in turn commit to making disciples who make disciples across social networks in the real world and the cyberworld—at school, on sports teams, in school clubs, at work, and everywhere you go. But it all starts with sharing Jesus with one person.

If you've led someone to Christ recently, map out a plan in your journal entry today about how you can help that person become a disciple who shares their faith with others. (For example, share this book with your friend.) If you haven't led someone to Christ yet, think about that next person you want to reach with the gospel. Write that person's name down in your journal entry and think through how you want to begin reaching out to this friend relationally and relentlessly.

My prayer and plan for exponential impact...

28 *twenty-eight*

MAKE IT | A TEAM EFFORT

Two people are better off than one, for they can help each other succeed. If one person falls, the other can reach out and help. But someone who falls alone is in real trouble…A person standing alone can be attacked and defeated, but two can stand back-to-back and conquer. Three are even better, for a triple-braided cord is not easily broken. **(Ecclesiastes 4:9-10, 12)**

THE BIG IDEA
Sharing your faith has its ups and downs, so actively seek out some Christian friends to walk this road with you.

LISTEN IN
There have been times when I've wanted to quit sharing my faith, but my best friend won't let me give up. My friend has given me Bible verses to encourage me. And together, we're living THE Cause and have started a Christian group at our school, as well as a Monday morning prayer group and a twice a week lunch Bible study.
—Tabetha

GO DEEPER
As you've shared your faith over these past days and weeks, there have probably been times when you've felt like Tabetha and wanted to throw in the towel. Maybe your popularity has taken a hit. Maybe you've felt inadequate or ineffective. Maybe someone's mocked you. Or maybe you just feel overwhelmed because this job Jesus has given you of making disciples is a *big* job.

Even Jesus' handpicked, personally trained first disciples faced difficulties and discouragement as they shared the gospel. In fact, 10 out of his first 12 disciples died martyrs' deaths for sharing their faith. So you're in good company if you're feeling some heat.

Knowing that challenges go with the territory of living THE Cause, what can you do that will help you stick with it? Of course you can't share Jesus without Jesus, so be sure you stay plugged into the power of the Holy Spirit through prayer and reading the Bible. Another major source of strength and encouragement for you is other Christian friends who will walk the road with you! As Ecclesiastes 4 describes, two or three helping each other are far stronger than one alone. You can share insights and ideas with each other and maybe even play tag team with the friends you're trying to reach. So seek out some Christian friends to do this reaching out thing with you! Together, you can hold each other accountable and encourage one another.

DO SOMETHING!

Don't try to go it alone. Who could you recruit to help you on this disciple-making journey? Spend some time journaling about how you might go about finding others who are willing to join you in your efforts to reach your school, your team, your community, or wherever God is calling you. You might also approach your youth leader to explore ideas for making outreach a team effort in your youth group. This could range from something as simple as asking your youth leader to give the gospel every week at youth group, to setting aside five minutes per meeting for teenagers to share stories up front about their efforts to share their faith, including not just the successes, but "the good, the bad, and the ugly."

And finally, get connected online to others committed to living THE Cause by joining the Live THE Cause fan page at Facebook.com/livethecause. It's loaded with interactive encouragement and ideas for sharing your faith!

My prayer and plan for making THE
Cause a team effort...

29 *twenty-nine*

SHARING JESUS
is a journey

Listen! A farmer went out to plant some seed. As he scattered it across his field, some of the seed fell on a footpath, and the birds came and ate it. Other seed fell on shallow soil with underlying rock. The seed sprouted quickly because the soil was shallow. But the plant soon wilted under the hot sun, and since it didn't have deep roots, it died. Other seed fell among thorns that grew up and choked out the tender plants so they produced no grain. Still other seeds fell on fertile soil, and they sprouted, grew, and produced a crop that was thirty, sixty, and even a hundred times as much as had been planted! **(Mark 4:3-8)**

THE BIG IDEA
Not everyone we share the gospel with will instantly become a Christian, but keep praying, pursuing, and persuading because you never know when the seeds you sow may finally take root.

LISTEN IN
Daniel and I were best friends from middle school on. Through the years, I talked with him about God again and again—after movies, during sleepovers, whenever and wherever. He'd frequently join me at youth group for our crazy-fun Capture the Flag games—though he was mostly there for the girls and the games. During high school, I invited him to our weekly Young Life meetings where he heard about Jesus again and again. And my parents talked about God with him repeatedly, since we spent a lot of time hanging at my house.

Well, high school graduation came and went, and we headed off to college in different states, but still we stayed in touch. The years passed, and we finished college, got jobs, and visited each other when we could. Now we're 24.

Recently, I got the most amazing phone call from my friend. "I've spent a lot of time thinking about it, and I've become a Christian," he told me. My jaw dropped. More than 10 years after I first started talking to him about spiritual things, the message of Christianity finally got through to him and he let God into his life. —Caleb

GO DEEPER

Jesus reminds his disciples in Mark 4 that not everyone we talk to about the gospel is going to be instantly all in for Jesus. So don't be discouraged if your attempts to share your faith are sometimes met with rolling eyes or cold shoulders. Jesus tells us to expect that some people will have no interest in God now or ever. But also remember that while one person's journey to Jesus might be a short trip, another's may take years and years. So don't give up on your friends who are on a longer journey to Jesus! Keep loving and listening. Keep praying, pursuing, and persuading. You never know when the seeds you plant might finally take root. It may take one day or 10 years or longer. Just keep living THE Cause out loud.

DO SOMETHING!

In your journal entry today, make a list of all the friends you can remember having spiritual conversations with. Update your Cause Circle to reflect what's been happening. Think about what your next step with each of these friends might look like. Jot down some ideas in your journal. Then step out and act on one of those ideas today.

So far I've talked to...

and my next step is...

thirty

LIVE | THE CAUSE

I pray that from his glorious, unlimited resources he will empower you with inner strength through his Spirit. Then Christ will make his home in your hearts as you trust in him. Your roots will grow down into God's love and keep you strong. And may you have the power to understand, as all God's people should, how wide, how long, how high, and how deep his love is. May you experience the love of Christ, though it is too great to understand fully. Then you will be made complete with all the fullness of life and power that comes from God. **(Ephesians 3:16-19)**

THE BIG IDEA

You need God's love and power in your life in order to live THE Cause every day.

LISTEN IN

Any place where teenagers work together with the same purpose can be transformed by God. Faith can move mountains, and the truth will set you free. I believe we can change the world. If we stop worrying about what other people will think about us and let go of the fear of rejection, God will captivate us and set us on fire for him. Together, driven by the Holy Spirit and empowered by God, we are unstoppable.

THE Cause is a great way to go about this. I challenge myself and every teenager in the world who has the truth of God in their hearts, to do something to help THE Cause. We all have a responsibility to share the good news. For me, I'm going to talk to someone different every day at my school. Every relationship will be so much more important. I will be bothered if even one of my friends doesn't have a relationship with Christ. It might be tough, but with God all things are possible. So, what are YOU going to do for THE Cause? —Rachel

GO DEEPER

So knowing how wide, how long, how high, and how deep Jesus' love for you is, are you committed to THE Cause for the long haul? Are you all in? Jesus put his life on the line for you. Are you ready to live for him?

Some Christian teenagers live their lives from spiritual high to spiritual high. They go to a camp, retreat, or conference and come away pumped up from their mountaintop experience. But after a few weeks back in the real world, that spiritual high ebbs and their commitment to Jesus fades away to background noise. Spiritual highs are great, but what's needed for the long haul is an ongoing infusion of God's power through his Holy Spirit. How do you get that? Through prayer and through his Word.

DO SOMETHING!

Read the Bible verses at the top of this entry again. Then write a note to God letting him know where you are on all this. Be honest—God knows your heart. If you're all in and eager to live for God and his cause—THE Cause—tell him that. If you're not, give God permission to get a hold of your heart so that it breaks for the lost, just as his did. In Ephesians 3:16 Paul says this: *I pray that from his glorious, unlimited resources he will empower you with inner strength through his Spirit.* Put that prayer into your own words. Then tap into God's mighty power through the Spirit and live THE Cause today and every day in your own unique way and for his glory. Get out there and rock your world for Jesus!

Dear God...

Check out where Dare 2 Share's teen training conference is going to be next www.dare2share.org/events

Inspire. Equip. Unleash.

"You experience firsthand how God can use you to reach others, even strangers. It is amazing what this two-day conference did for me and my friends. God changed us and challenged us in ways that we thought were impossible. We went home ready to change the world."

- Bethany

 Join the conversation!

Share stories, and encouragement for THE Cause

www.facebook.com/livethecause

More books from Dare 2 Share

Share your faith through story

Check out this quick read and then pass it on to your friends. *Venti Jesus Please* tells the story of three friends - an atheist, agnostic, and Christian - and their honest spiritual conversation at their local Starbucks.

Jared is an atheist with an attitude.

Kailey is a new believer with a temper.

Follow the story of their senior year and find out what can happen when just one teen is passionate about the mission of Jesus to reach the lost.

Share your faith with anyone, anytime, anywhere!

Dare 2 Share: A Field Guide will help you discover your own unique sharing style, plus provides you with profiles of various belief systems and tips on how to bring your faith up without throwing up.

Available at www.Dare2Share.org

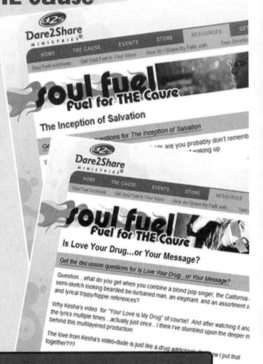